NORTH AMERICAN ANIMALS

Canada Geese

by Megan Borgert-Spaniol

BLASTOFF!
READERS
3

BELLWETHER MEDIA · MINNEAPOLIS, MN

Note to Librarians, Teachers, and Parents:

Blastoff! Readers are carefully developed by literacy experts and combine standards-based content with developmentally appropriate text.

Level 1 provides the most support through repetition of high-frequency words, light text, predictable sentence patterns, and strong visual support.

Level 2 offers early readers a bit more challenge through varied simple sentences, increased text load, and less repetition of high-frequency words.

Level 3 advances early-fluent readers toward fluency through increased text and concept load, less reliance on visuals, longer sentences, and more literary language.

Level 4 builds reading stamina by providing more text per page, increased use of punctuation, greater variation in sentence patterns, and increasingly challenging vocabulary.

Level 5 encourages children to move from "learning to read" to "reading to learn" by providing even more text, varied writing styles, and less familiar topics.

Whichever book is right for your reader, Blastoff! Readers are the perfect books to build confidence and encourage a love of reading that will last a lifetime!

This edition first published in 2017 by Bellwether Media, Inc.

No part of this publication may be reproduced in whole or in part without written permission of the publisher. For information regarding permission, write to Bellwether Media, Inc., Attention: Permissions Department, 5357 Penn Avenue South, Minneapolis, MN 55419.

Library of Congress Cataloging-in-Publication Data

Names: Borgert-Spaniol, Megan, 1989- author.
Title: Canada Geese / by Megan Borgert-Spaniol.
Other titles: Blastoff! Readers. 3, North American Animals.
Description: Minneapolis, MN : Bellwether Media, Inc., [2017] | Series:
    Blastoff! Readers. North American Animals | Audience: Ages 5-8. |
    Audience: K to grade 3. | Includes bibliographical references and index.
Identifiers: LCCN 2015046394 | ISBN 9781626174016 (hardcover : alk. paper)
Subjects: LCSH: Canada goose–Behavior–Juvenile literature. | Canada
    goose–Juvenile literature.
Classification: LCC QL696.A52 B675 2017 | DDC 598.4/178–dc23
LC record available at http://lccn.loc.gov/2015046394

Table of
Contents

What Are Canada Geese?   4

Finding Food   8

Flocks   12

Nesting   16

Goslings   20

Glossary   22

To Learn More   23

Index   24

What Are Canada Geese?

Canada geese are large birds with long necks.

N
W E
S

Canada geese range = ⬛

conservation status: least concern

Extinct

Extinct in the Wild

Critically Endangered

Endangered

Vulnerable

Near Threatened

Least Concern

They are found throughout most of North America. They live near ponds, rivers, and other bodies of water.

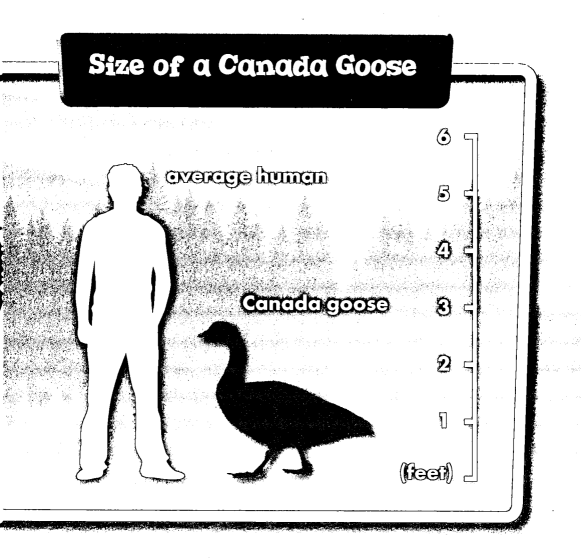

Size of a Canada Goose

average human

Canada goose

6
5
4
3
2
1
(feet)

These birds stand about 3 feet (1 meter) tall. They measure about 5 feet (1.5 meters) from one wing tip to the other.

Canada geese are good swimmers. They have large **webbed feet** that help them move through water.

Canada geese are **herbivores**. They eat grasses, seeds, and berries.

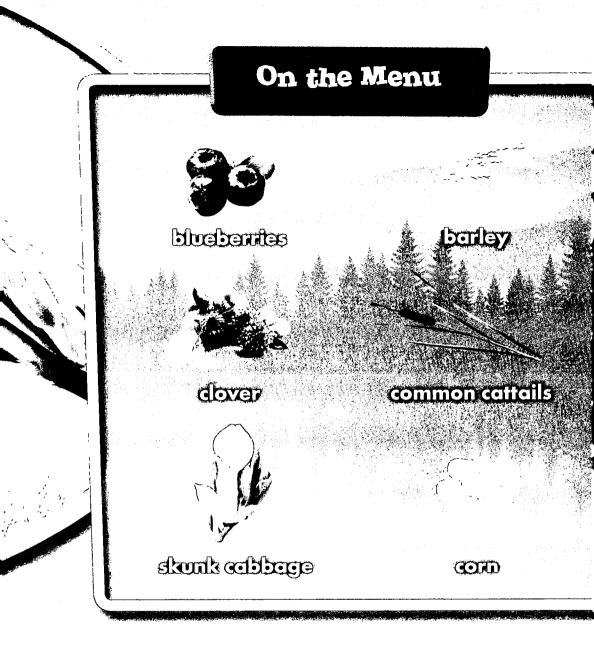

On the Menu

blueberries

barley

clover

common cattails

skunk cabbage

corn

Their bills have tiny tooth-like edges that make it easy to cut food.

Identify a Canada Goose

large body   **webbed feet**   **white chin**

The geese **graze** in fields, parks, and large lawns.

They also feed on **aquatic** plants.
They tip upside down and reach
their necks underwater to find
plants to eat.

Canada geese travel in **flocks** most of the year. Members of a flock call to one another with loud honks.

The geese stay together in flat, open areas. This makes it easier to spot **predators**.

Some flocks **migrate** south for winter. They fly in the shape of a "V." This helps them travel far and fast.

A flock can travel 1,500 miles
(2,400 kilometers) in one day!

In spring, pairs of male and female geese leave the flock to **breed**.

A female builds a nest out of plants, twigs, and feathers. After she lays eggs, she sits on the nest to keep them warm.

Animals to Avoid

bald eagles

coyotes

bobcats

red foxes

The male guards the nest against crows and other predators. He also keeps other geese away.

The parents lower their necks and hiss if predators come too close.

Goslings

Goslings hatch about one month later. They can walk and swim within a day or two. Goslings can fly after about 7 weeks. Soon they will fly with the flock!

Baby Facts

Name for babies:	goslings
Number of eggs laid:	2 to 10 eggs
Time spent inside egg:	about 1 month
Time spent with parents:	about 1 year

Glossary

aquatic—grows in water

breed—to produce offspring

flocks—groups of Canada geese that travel and graze together

goslings—baby Canada geese

graze—to eat grasses and other plants on the ground

herbivores—animals that eat only plants

migrate—to travel from one place to another, often with the seasons

predators—animals that hunt other animals for food

webbed feet—feet with thin skin that connects the toes

To Learn More

AT THE LIBRARY

Alderfer, Jonathan K. *National Geographic Kids Bird Guide of North America: The Best Birding Book for Kids from National Geographic's Bird Experts.* Washington, D.C.: National Geographic, 2013.

Best, Cari. *Goose's Story.* New York, N.Y.: Farrar, Straus and Giroux, 2002.

Sayre, April Pulley. *Honk, Honk, Goose! Canada Geese Start a Family.* New York, N.Y.: Henry Holt, 2009.

ON THE WEB

Learning more about Canada geese is as easy as 1, 2, 3.

1. Go to www.factsurfer.com.

2. Enter "Canada geese" into the search box.

3. Click the "Surf" button and you will see a list of related web sites.

With factsurfer.com, finding more information is just a click away.

Index

bills, 9

breed, 16

call, 12

eggs, 17, 21

female, 16, 17

flocks, 12, 14, 15, 16, 20

fly, 14, 20

food, 8, 9, 11

goslings, 20, 21

graze, 10

hatch, 20

herbivores, 8

hiss, 19

honks, 12

male, 16, 18

migrate, 14

necks, 4, 11, 19

nest, 17, 18

ponds, 5

predators, 13, 18, 19

range, 5

rivers, 5

seasons, 14, 16

size, 4, 6

swimmers, 7, 20

travel, 12, 14, 15

water, 5, 7, 11

webbed feet, 7, 10

wing, 6

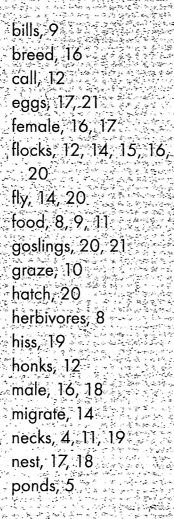